HOW YOU CAN BE DISCIPLINED WITH YOUR SAVINGS

BY

DANNY GEORGE AWAIKO

Danny George Awaiko

LEGAL DISCLAIMER

Published in Nigeria by
DANGOFE PUBLISHING HOUSE
3 Duenta Street, Abuloma,
Port-Harcourt, Rivers State Nigeria.
TEL: +23408063689774, +23408056738866
Email: dannygeorge002@yahoo.com

ISBN: 9798715332134

TABLE OF CONTENT

Dedication

This book is dedicated to my wife Glory, and Juanita my daughter.

Chapter One

When you have easy access to your savings

In my years of existence as a young man, I have come to the conclusion that the major problem we are facing as individuals when it comes to finance is not how to save money, but how to be discipline with our savings. There is no denial to the fact that most persons can save money but the truth still remains that they are not discipline with their savings, most especially when they have easy access to it. Let me narrate a story to prove my point.

A young lady decided to save #5,000 (Nigerian currency) on a monthly basis so she can pay her school fees and buy at least some books at the resumption of school. She set duration of one year to meet this target. This means at the end of 12 months she must have saved #60,000. She commenced the savings project January that year with December of that year as maturity date. She was initially doing very well but tampered with the money after ten months of savings. She used the money for irrelevant issues which included borrowing the money to her siblings who used it for a business adventure that never saw the light of the day. The conclusion of the whole matter is that she never went back to school because she lacked the discipline to save money.

When I did my investigation on her story, I discovered that she was saving her money in the bank. I also discovered that the money was not on any saving plan or fixed deposit, but was just deposited in the bank. This is why withdrawing the money to give to her sibling was not a big deal. I am not implying you should not assist your sibling if you have the money or deposit money in the bank. If you are saving for a purpose please stick to it that is the discipline we are talking about. You must be focused to actualize your saving goals. On the other hand, your savings should not be kept in the bank as idle money without a saving plan, because you can access it easily. There are other platforms still in the bank that you can safe lock your money. I can recommend one for you if you contact me. Furthermore, every other money you want to use to pay your day to day bills can be left in the bank.

The story of the lady above is an example of what most of us are doing today when it comes to saving money. We have the passion to save money but lack the discipline or the skill to keep the savings till the maturity date.

Are you saving to start a business? Are you saving for your wedding? Are you planning to go back to school? Are you saving to write a professional exam? Or you are saving to pay your rent. Please I want you to focus on most of the things I will be saying in this book, because it will help you not to repeat the samemistakes you made in your last saving plan.

Chapter Two

Things You Must Consider Before You Start Saving Money

There are things I personally consider before i start any savings plan. In this chapter I will be sharing them with you, and am sure it will be of great assistance as you commence your own savings.

Consider the starting and maturity date of your savings

Any saving plan that does not have a commencement and a maturity date is not genuine. If you just want to save money without a purpose, then you will end up frustrated at the end of the day. This is because you don't have a focus and your target plans are not in place. Show me a man who will smile at the end of the day with his savings and I will show you a man who has a commencement and a maturity date for his savings.

How can you save money when you don't know the maturity date for that savings? That means you don't even have any plans for the money in the first place, you were only saving without a purpose.

A young man had a 3 years saving planned to buy a car. He stated the 1st day the savings will commence, the amount to be saved on monthly basis and the maturity date. It will interest you to note that he bought that car at the end of 3 years. However, he was disciplined with his savings for this 3 years and one of the things that helped him to sustain his discipline was because he never had easy access to his savings. I will be discussing the principles that will help you to be disciplined with your savings as we proceed in the next chapter.

Save money with a purpose

One of the blunders you can make when it comes to saving, is when you start saving without a purpose. Saving without a purpose can be an hindrance as far as your saving plan is concerned. I can never start any saving plan without a purpose. Your purpose of saving that money is what will give you the booster to save more. Your purpose of saving that money must be spelt out from the very onset.

Another irony is when you are saving for a particular thing and end up using the money for something else. You have just succeeded in betraying yourself. I assure you that next time you will repeat the same thing and end up without results. This is one of the major reasons why we have so many abandoned projects, but we have been saving. Stick to the purpose of saving that money. I cannot tamper with my daughter's education savings because I am hungry or because someone has been on my neck to pay her house rent. We are talking about my daughter's future here. I am not disputing the fact that if I had extra money apart from my savings I will not assist in paying the house rent of course I will. The point I am trying to make is that until you stick to the purpose of saving that money, you will never accomplish any targeted goal in life. Give your savings a direction.

What are you saving for? Give it a name now. Are you saving money for your rent, education, wedding, business, car, or name it. There must be a purpose to why you are saving that money. You don't just save money because you want to. You might end-up using that money for so many irrelevant things. Let me summarize this point by saying that: saving without a purpose is a wasted effort...

Consider the institution

It is obvious that most persons have lost their money in the past; because of the institution they saved their money.

Before you embark on saving your money with any financial institution, first of all consider the present status of that institution. Don't be carried away by their past records. Their past records might mislead you into losing your money in the name of savings. Knowing the history of the financial institution is also important but we are talking about how reliable they are today. Can they give you back your money at the maturity date without any stories? This is one of the basic questions you should ask yourself.

Let me also admit this fact, for those of you who like saving your money in the hands of individuals in the name of "contributions", I hope you will not develop high blood pressure when they disappear into the thin air with your money. So many persons have been victims, please don't be the next.

Categorize your savings

Another thing you need to consider before you start saving your money is to agree within yourself, if you are saving for a short-term, medium-term, or a long term goal. This will help you to a great extent in your saving plan. Don't just save aimlessly.

Chapter Three

Principles that will help you to be disciplined with your savings

In this chapter we would be looking at certain values that can help you to be disciplined with your savings, only if you start the application today.

1. See your savings as your future pay-off

The moment you start seeing your savings as your future pay-off, it will help you to maintain a high level of discipline.

It will be a thing of joy peradventure you lose your job tomorrow and you suddenly realize that the money you have been saving for the past ten years is almost due for maturity. There will be no need for you to develop high blood pressure because you lost your job. Thinking about what to do and where to start from should not be a problem. All you need to do is to harvest your savings that is due and invest in a business.

This is very important because most persons have died in their 60s, 70s, and even 50s, because they ate their seed and harvest when things were going on well for them. They never set-aside any savings plan that will serve as a pay-off for them after retirement.

A man I know too well spent many years working for a multi-national company in Nigeria died few months after his retirement from his company. This sad incidence occurred because he had nothing to fall back to. He never prepared any savings that will serve as a pay-off for him after retirement. While others were busy saving for the future, he was busy lavishing his money on women, cars, and all manner of irrelevant things. He eventually developed high blood pressure and died.

The worst thing that can happen to any man is to consume the future today. This is one of the major problems I have with this present generation of young men and women. They never seem to learn from the mistakes of those who have gone ahead of them. They don't care about the future; they don't care about savings or investment, thy end up eating their future today.

2. Safelock your savings

One of the fastest growing ways you can be disciplined with your savings is to safe-lock your savings. It has been tested and trusted and I have used this method so many times and it worked perfectly well for me.

What is safelocking?

It is a short-term investment plan or platform that allows you to earn interest upfront when you lock away a portion of your savings for a fixed period. e.g.
- PIGGY BANK

Safe-locking your savings will not only help you to save money, but also to get interest from your savings at the maturity date.

I am not so concerned about the interest you get from it, but the discipline it helps you to maintain. It is obvious that whenever you Safe-lock your savings you will find it difficult to have access to funds. After all, you have an ultimate reason why you are saving that money; not for every other reason.

There are so many banks that can help you to Safe-lock your savings for a given period of time. It all depends on what you want. You can Safe-lock your money for 30 days, 60 days, 90 days or even one year, or as the case may be. This is a sure disciplinary measure that will help you not to break your saving box anytime you like.

3. Plan your expenses according to your income

The secret of savings is spending below your income. So many persons are in debt today because they will never plan their expenses according to their earnings. When you are not prudent with your financial transactions according to your income, the next thing that comes to mind is to start looking for how to tamper with your savings.

So many persons are wasteful; they spend money buying so many irrelevant things that is not necessary. And at the end of the day, they will look for where to borrow. In a situation where they cannot borrow from any source, the next thing that comes to mind is their savings which in most cases has not gotten to the maturity date for usage. Some people engage in emotional purchase which is buying without a plan or off budget.

I met a lady years ago who's monthly income as at then was forty thousand naira (#40,000). In one of the months she decided to purchase hair attachment worth forty thousand naira on collecting her salary that same month. Of course this same lady had to borrow money to foot other bills since she had already used her entire income just for hair. I was looking at the foolishness and the stupidity she displayed as she was narrating the story to me. How can someone with senses use all her monthly income just for one item?It is amazing, isn't it?

If you must harvest your savings at the maturity date, then you must learn how to plan your budget according to your income. You must subject yourself to discipline. You must also differentiate your needs from your wants. You must not buy the latest phone, shoes, bags, cars, all at once. Tomorrow is another day. Am not saying getting the latest version of those items I mentioned is bad. However, you must apply wisdom with your income so that you will not be thinking of how to break your saving box all the time.

Below is a proposed template that can give you a helping hand each time you receive any income.

S/N	Financial plan	Percentages
1	Tithe	10%
2	Covenant seed	10%
3	Savings	20%
4	investment	10%
5	Other expenses	50%
6	Total	100%

Analysis of items on the template

Tithe and covenant seed

I think it will not be out of place if you pay your tithe as a Christian and also set aside an offering to God, I believe that is the right thing to do.

Savings

If you must have an assurance of your future, then you must learn how to set aside at least 20% of every income that comes in.

Investment

Every wise man will always want to venture into any business or the purchase of assets that can bring additional money in future. At least you need to set aside 10% from every income to accumulate money for investment.

Expenses

I cannot dictate to you how to spend 50% of your income for expenses. But you need to consider the basic necessities like: food clothing, shelter, etc.

With this template you can plan your expenses very well according to your income, without tampering with your already existing savings. Am not saying you must use this template, you can also develop your own. I only used it as a guide to help you maintain a high level of discipline with your inflow.

4. Save your money for things that can be disposed easily without losing value

From my experience, one of the ways you can be disciplined with your savings is to save your money for things that can be disposed easily when you need the money. Not just anything but things that can also increase in value as time goes on.

For instance, I decided to exchange the money I was saving for my daughter on a particular gift item on recharge cards, knowing fully well that the value of recharge cards will not depreciate; rather it will appreciate whenever there is scarcity. Interestingly, I don't want to save this money in the bank.If you have Fifty thousand naira and you don't want to use any other method to save the money, you can simply buy recharge card of different networks, valued at Fifty thousand naira, and keep it in your drawer. When it is getting close to the maturity date of when you need the money, you can simply sell the recharge cards and get back the Fifty thousand naira with interest. You will notice that a high level of discipline has just been maintained, because you don't have access to cash until you sell the recharge cards and get back the money you were saving.

Not only can you save your money on recharge cards, there are also many things you can save your money on, just in case you don't want to use the banks and other saving platforms.Another good example is to buy a virgin land in a promising environment. The value of a land can never depreciate; rather it will continue to appreciate as time goes on.

For instance, if you have #2,000,000.00 (Two million naira), that you want to save for the next 5 years for a future investment, and you don't want to save it in the bank or any other savings platform; you can decide to buy a virgin land with that same amount of money. You will be amazed that after 5 years the value of the land has appreciated. You will not only get back your money after selling the land. You are also sure of extra money, because the value of the land has appreciated.

However, the most important thing is that you have been able to maintain a high level of discipline by not tampering with the two million naira you saved for your future investment, which was actually the main target. With these examples you can at least choose anything to exchange your savings with, provided it is something that will not make your savings to lose value.

5. Do not leave idle money in your account in the name of savings

I have made it clear to most persons around me who care to listen, that I don't keep idle money in the bank in the name of savings. It is either I safelock the money, put it on a fixed deposit, or I invest the money on any meaningful business.

The reason is because, when you keep your money in the bank in the name of savings, you will lack that discipline to allow that savings to get to the maturity date. What about the bank charges you receive every now and then? Don't you think it will have a little effect on your lumped-up savings at the maturity date? On the other hand, you will end up withdrawing your savings for so many irrelevant things because you have access to cash.

With these illustrations, you will agree with me that keeping idle money in the bank in the name of savings should be highly discouraged. You can use every other method I have already explained in this book to save your money.

6. Stay away from panic/emotional buying

If there is anything that has made so many persons break their saving box, it is panic buying.

What is panic buying?

1) It is the action of buying large quantities of a particular product or commodity due to sudden fears of a forthcoming shortage or price rise.

2) Panic buying occurs when consumers buy unusually large amounts of a product in anticipation of, or after disaster or perceived disaster or anticipation of large price increase or shortage.- **Oxford Languages Dictionary**

3) A situation where so many people buy as much food, fuel, etc. As they can because they are worried about something bad that may happen- **Cambridge Dictionary**

If you must be disciplined with your savings, then avoid anything that has to do with panic buying. This you must do because you will end up breaking your saving box. Have you not noticed that each time you engage in panic induced purchases, you end up not using those things at the long –run or buying at higher prices than you should? The annoying part of it is that some of the items we buy do to panic are perishable in nature. We also suffer losses of these products due to expiration dates because we did not bother to check them during purchase as a result of fear and rush. You have just succeeded in wasting money, including the one in your saving box. After all you never planned for the buying.

I don't believe in panic buying, because there is no sense in it. I can imagine myself stocking things I don't need because of the fear of the unknown or some rumors emanating from self-aggrandized people who want to capitalize on the human fear to make extra money. This is my own opinion.

Some persons even stock petrol in their houses due to fear of scarcity, thereby exposing the entire neighborhood to risk.

However, the most important thing is that, if we must maintain a high level of discipline with our savings, then panic buying should be one of the things we must stay away from.

Please don't quote me wrong,am not saying you should not stock your house with products but wisdom should be applied in this matter.

7. Break from the camp of indisciplined persons

If you must maintain a high level of discipline with your savings, then you have to make up your mind to disconnect yourself from indisciplined persons. If you have friends who are never satisfied with what they have, spending money unnecessarily, and tampering with their savings every now and then. Watch-out, very soon you will do the same. So the best time to break from that camp is now. I can't parade myself with friends who don't care about the future, who only care about how they will lavish their savings today. They end up eating their future today. They spend money on the latest phones, cars, shoes, cloths, etc. I will never have any business with someone who will always spend 50% of his income in the beer parlor in the name of enjoyment.

Few years ago, I disconnected myself from a colleague whom I discovered was never disciplined with his finance. I noticed each time he received his salary, the first thing that comes to his mind is the buying of shoes, cloths, and electronics. You will never hear him talking about how to save or invest any money. Such kind of friends should not be found around you if you must maintain a disciplined financial life style. Am not saying that buying all these things is wrong, but wisdom is profitable to direct in issues like this.

8. Always plan your buying

Each time you don't plan your buying, watch it, the next place you will want to pay a visit to is your savings. This is reality because I have seen so many persons collecting money from their savings when it has not gotten to the maturity date. Perhaps they saw the latest car, phone, cloths, shoes, wristwatches, etc.this act is usually perpetrated more by the female folk. How can you start buying things you did not plan for? It is either you collect money from your savings or you will end up in debts. This is the indiscipline am talking about. The funny aspect of it is that, most of the items are kept in the house for years without any usage.

I once visited a young lady where I saw plenty of shoes in her house numbering 50-70 pairs. I asked her, what are you doing with all these shoes? In her response she told me that each time she is moving with her friends on the road, they like buying the latest shoes. So for her not to be left out, she will equally do same, thereby owing debts and removing money from her savings. Do you now see the reason why I said you should break from the camp of indisciplined folks? They will lead you to buy things you never planned or have no use for. Try and make friends with persons who have maintained a disciplined life style. It will help you not only in your savings, but also in other aspects of life. Disconnect yourself from every unserious, undisciplined associate.

Definition of major Terms Used

Savings

- The money you put aside for future use rather than spending it immediately.
- It refers to the amount left over after an individual's consumer spending is subtracted form the amount of disposable income earned in a given period of time.

Discipline

- It refers to instruction and training.
- It can also be defined from the Cambridge English dictionary as the ability to control yourself or other people, even in difficult situations.

ABOUT THE BOOK

The major problem we are facing as individuals when it comes to finance is not how to save money, but how to be disciplined with our savings. There is no denial to the fact that most persons can save money but the truth still remains that they are not disciplined with their savings, most especially when they have easy access to it.

This book presents to you certain principles that have been tested and trusted to help you become disciplined with your savings.If you adhere to these principles I assure you that you will smile at the end of every saving plan.

About The Author

Danny George Awaiko *is anapostle of Revival, a Preacher, a Motivational Speaker, and a man who loves the Holy Spirit. He also shares his insight with singles. He is a self-publishing author, and has written several inspirational books like: 10 Steps to Become a Champion, Sex Without Knowledge, 21 Ways to Identify False Prophets, 7 killing D's Of Destiny, 7 Catalyst of Revival, 24 Secrets of Worship, 7 Spirits Militating Against The Church,21 Reasons Why you are Hot and still Single and many others.*

For 14 years, he has impacted on so many youths in different higher institutions and churches. His first book, "The Secret Is Out", has reached out to many lives. He is a mindset coach, a personal development speaker, and a financial analyst. Danny volunteers to aid the campaign against the abuseof the girl child. He is a conference speaker. Danny lives in Abuja, Nigeria and loves writing, reading, fitness and travelling.

Other Books By: Danny George Awaiko

1) The Secret Is Out
2) How to attain 100% performance in your business.
3) Holy Spirit my best friend
4) 24 secrets of worship
5) 21 Ways to Identify False Prophets
6) 7 killing D'S OF Destiny
7) 7 Catalyst of Revival
8) Destiny plucked out of fire
9) 10 Steps to become a Champion.
10) Checklist for Savings and Investment

11) Sex without knowledge

12) The Myth about Sex

SHORT STORIES

1) Amanda and the wicked queen

2) Mind the company you keep

3) The Noisy Neighbor

4) No sweat-No Sweet

5) The window and the wise dog

Connect With Me

Thank you for buying and reading this book, please remember to leave reviews and connect with me on social media platforms:

Email: dannygeorge002@yahoo.com

Facebook: @ dannygeorge

Twitter: @ dannygeorge

Mobile Number:

±23408063689774...